AN
INCARNATION
OF THE
SNOW

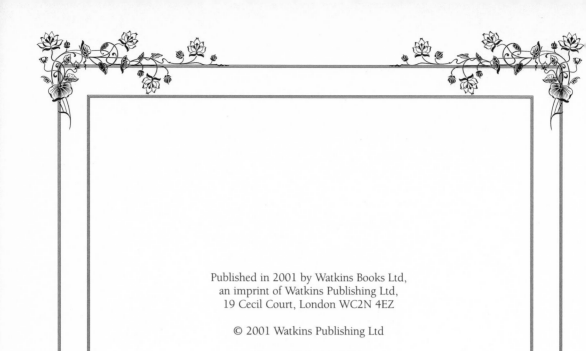

Published in 2001 by Watkins Books Ltd,
an imprint of Watkins Publishing Ltd,
19 Cecil Court, London WC2N 4EZ

First published in 1903

Designed and produced for Watkins Books
by Open Door Limited
Edited by Mary Morton

Title: An Incarnation of the Snow
ISBN: 1 84293 000 1

The Indian Stories of F. W. Bain

AN
INCARNATION
OF THE
SNOW

WATKINS

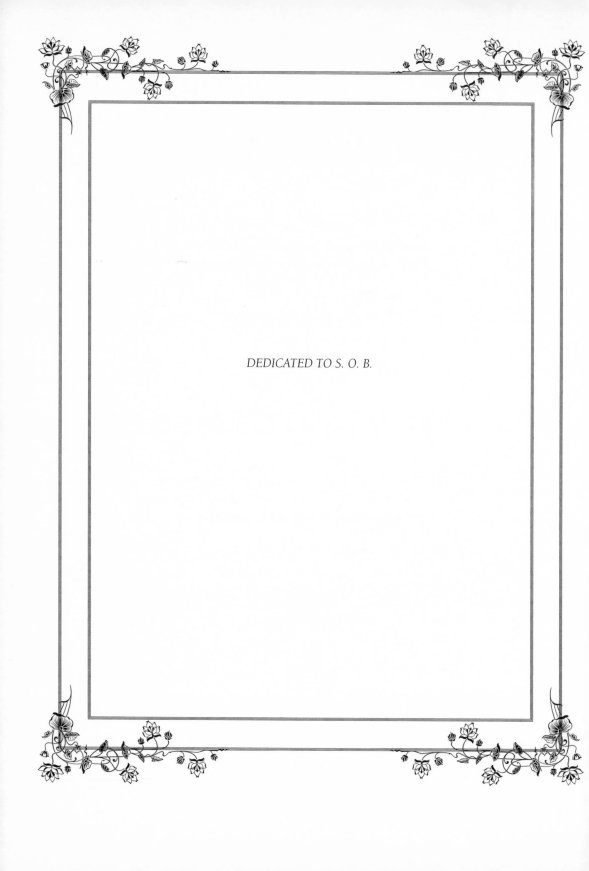

DEDICATED TO S. O. B.

(भवमानसालयाज्योत्ला)

भवानेभामिजगत्तमोऴ्ली सुधाद्रवामिस्ररतापशान्त्यै
महोर्मिमार्गानिसदाचरामि संसारभग्नाश्चितोद्कानि

I flash and glow on Being's Brow, and my snow-cold

Ooze is Love's life-blood,

And I wander over the Waves of Time, where the

World-wrack drifts in my Silver Flood

भवौसमुत्पन्नविलम्भवादौ श्रितौ सरोजैः कलहंसदूहैः

And the moonflowers hear, on the far blue Mere

Where only the wild swans go,

What the Great God whispers into the ear

Of the Daughter of the Snow

CONTENTS

PREFACE

ARTARY says the Abbé Huc – himself the most imaginative and inimitable of all wanderers – is peopled with pilgrim birds: 'high up in air, you see them roam, in dense battalions, forming in their flight, with a kind of drill in its caprice, a thousand quaint designs, which melt away only to be formed anew.' So also, that region of vast and melancholy plains, stretching and rising southward ever to the white wall of huge Himálaya, is the very home of lakes: 'Koko Nurs': blue lovely sheets of sapphire, scattered like fragments of a broken mirror to spot earth with the colour of the sky. And one of these, hidden away in the all but inaccessible snows just south of Kailàs – where the Great God dwells – is the sacred Mountain Tarn, Mánasa: and thereby hangs our tale, whose title is so idiomatic that it can be rendered into English only by a paraphrase, losing a little of its Indian aroma on the way. It says to us this: What the Swan is to the Lake, what the Moon is to the Sky, what Párwatí – the Daughter of Himálaya – is to her Lord, that is woman to the world: the Haunter, the Indweller, the Ornament, the Fixed Idea, the Mystic Solitary Swan in the heart of the dark blue lake of Time.

There would be more than a grain of truth in the assertion, that all old Hindoo literature is little but a long hymn to the Moon. It moves in a lunar atmosphere, found nowhere else on earth; a

strange holy twilight, suggestive of another world. Nothing is so dreamy, so utterly remote from everyday reality, as this enchanted, ghostly air. And yet it is easily intelligible, since the normal condition of those who live in it is the occasional experience of every common mortal. For who has not, now and then, fallen under the spell, and found himself, so to say, diabolically snared into the worship of the Moon? Who is there that has not felt that planetary influence, that magnetic, half mysterious attraction, that Lohengrinesque amalgam of dusky camphor and mountain snowflake, silver of swan and foam of sea, which oozes, as the Hindoos say, out of the evening moon? Nature can sing it to herself, by means of her magical creation, the voices of the nightingales, 'at shut of eve': but what articulate Endymion[1] could ever put his passion into words?

I well remember a moment when I was myself almost bewitched, the day the Prince of Wales arrived in India, in 1905.

On that auspicious morning, all was enthusiasm and tumult in Bombay. Viceroys and Rájás, dignitaries of all descriptions, civil or military, eastern or western, were jostling one another to do honour to the heir of Empire. There was to be found everybody in India who was anybody. But I, being unfortunately nobody, far away in the purple ghauts, had risen long before the sun, and in the pale cool shadowy dawn, while yet 'the faint east quickened,' I went obscure, down, down: down, past bushes of deep red shoeflower, glimmering out of dusky brakes: down by winding

[1] *'Quid est credere in Deum ?' asks S. Augustine, and he answers: 'credendo amare, credendo diligere, credendo in Eum ire et Ejus membris incorporari.' We have only to change the gender to see how narrow is the line that divides religious ecstasy from sexual emotion.*

leafy roads, past long ascending grunting files of early-rising nearly naked copper-coloured sons and daughters of the soil, bending under bowing loads of rustling grass that hid their heads: past giant cactus candlesticks, festooned with hanging chains of blue convolvulus, and perched where you might have dropped a stone suddenly into the tops of trees, a thousand feet below: past here and there a monster spray of white 'wild arrow-root,' standing, a little bent, alone with its own loveliness ineffable, against a background of the dark: down, down, by jagged rocky paths resembling what in fact they were, the dried-up beds of torrents, fit rather to be monkeys' ladders than ways for voice-dividing men: down, hour by hour, until at last the sun was high, and I came out into a steaming airless valley, through which a little brook ran babbling, its waters, clear as crystal, flashing with swarms of tiny minnows, so brightly, as to be almost painful to the eye. Then on along a white and glaring, dusty road, where flocks of emerald parrots shot and screamed about the trees: and then once more, up and up, by a dark and cool delicious forest path, like the very road to the bower of a Sleeping Beauty, and steeper than the way to heaven, till finally I gained the top, and stood within the old Marátha fort.

This old hill-fort, built of black, cyclopean blocks of basalt, whose every crevice holds a tiny fern of brightest green, juts out into the sky, on the very edge of a precipice, dropping on its western side almost perpendicularly down two thousand feet and

more. So there, on the very verge, between the rank red-yellow jungle growth that fills the deserted fort within, and the empty space, below, I lay as it were suspended, like Trishanku, in the air. And now, it was nearly noon. Great blue, metallic butterflies lazily floated by me: the jungle sighed and whispered, just behind me; and an insect, every now and then, flashed past my ear with a fierce and sudden hum, that was lost as soon as heard. Far down below, a hawk was hovering, motionless as in a picture. And every now and then, a pair of great white vultures, circling majestically about above the walls against the clear blue sky, startled me by the rushing roar of their outstretched, black-edged wings, as they swooped close beside me, one bright, keen, curious eye fixed on the strange intruder, who all the while was lying still, drinking in with ear and eye the menacing and sinister beauty of the wilderness of wild hills that lay, with silence brooding over them, red and barren and burned and blistered, far as the eye could see, north, west, and south: throbbing, as it were, and quivering, like some vast alembic of molten metal, changing colour in a bluish glare, or one of those old deserts produced by the 'enchantment' of some African magician in the old Arabian Nights of childhood, the only true Arabian Nights, that tell of lands no man knows where, beyond strange yellow seas.

And as I lay, sharing with the vultures the vast distance and the dizzy depth, the draught of the infinite, the old blessing of Joseph, in a far off Syrian land, suddenly rushed into my mind.[1] Here, on

[1]*Deut. xxxiii. 13. 'Blessed of the Lorde is his land, for the sweeteness of heaven, for the dewe, and for the depth lying beneath, And for the sweete increase of the sunne, and for the sweete increase of the moone, And for the sweetenesse of the top of the ancient mountaines, and for the sweetenesse of the olde hilles.'*

the tops of 'ancient hilles,' you seem to become endowed, like the old 'yogis,' with an extra sense, You seem to hear, as you lie and listen, the ticking of the Great Clock, and a faint echo of the spheres. Aye! Pátanjali was right. Those who listen habitually to silence, learn to hear voices, and a music far sweeter than any earthly strain.

And I looked north, towards Bombay, hidden away on the far horizon in the haze and glare. And I said: O Prince of Wales, who, of all that cross thy path in India, will either know or dare to tell thee the thing that is in India's heart, as she sits with face turned down and back, so utterly lost in worship of gods that the world has all forgotten that she cares for nothing else? 'Behold me, a withered trunk, how I have suddenly shot out with foreign foliage! I, who of old myself produced great store of fruit and leafy beauty, not a whit inferior to this. But let a man choose for his mistress one who will understand him and requite him even after he is dead.'[1] My heart is stifled. I want my own old gods, not yours: yours, that were only the child of mine. Your Protestant missionary is pure impertinence. Your frigid melancholy theism is a mere segment of my joyous mystical polytheism, which better reflects the many facets of an incomprehensible divinity. And Incarnation is not your idea, but mine. All that you come to teach me, I knew, better than even Egypt knew it, long before you ever were. For I also am a Holy Land: my very air is sacred; yet you send conceited cobblers and stupid wife-embracing parsons to teach me little isolated fragments of my own old mystic lore. As well might the Welsh hills come over sea to show Kailàs or Kanchanjunga what a mountain really is, or the Sáhara Marusthalí deem itself competent to teach botany to Brazil. Do men carry owls to Athens, or coals to Newcastle? What art was to the Greek, or policy to the Roman, or business is to London, that religion is to me. And if indeed religion is only nonsense, as your wise men say, then am I also less than nothing. But if not, then learn, once for all, that the Ganges is more sacred than the Thames, and that all the London churches contain less religion than Benares, where calm-eyed sages sat of old by the purifying water, repeating: 'One is the Deity, but the wise call him by many names': when Oxford and Cambridge were as yet homes only for the bittern and the snipe.

And then, after a while, I rose up and went away, down the hill and over the plain. And missing my true path, like Dante, I wandered about the jungle, many a mile astray: and now it was, that I was punished for my presumption, in venturing, though in indifferent health, to challenge the Sun God by a thirty mile walk, and do battle with him all day long in his own domain. For now he had me at advantage, compelling me, whether I would or no, to climb back into the haunts of men over a treeless, shadeless hill on which he beat with all his force, steep as the wall of a house. Twenty times I lay down, all but defeated, with a broken heart. And when at last I reached the top, I found my way blocked, as if

by his command, by a recent landslip, across whose face I had to pass, like a fly clinging to a pillar, about a thousand feet high, on pain of going back to the bottom and beginning all over again. Death itself would have been preferable.

I beat my enemy, but I shall never forget the climb. Used up, wet through, and trembling in every limb: so tired, that I think, had anyone spoken to me, I should have burst into tears, with a shout of laughter, I reached my own verandah, and fell into a chair. The world faded out of my mind: I sank, not into sleep, but a kind of waking swoon. And there as I lay, time slowly wore away, and little by little, the day died.

And all at once, as if someone had suddenly touched me, I came to myself. The sun was gone: the day was dead. Before me, still and cold and black, were the mighty shoulders of those cruel hills, over which I had come. Above them stretched the floor of heaven, deep violet overhead, pale, clear, transparent ochrous grey below, with here and there a star. All round me was the chirp of crickets, the chuckle of bed-going birds, dim darkness, leafy labyrinths: out of the shadow, every now and then, a night-jar rose, on noiseless velvet wing, hung for a single instant fluttering against the sky, and vanished like a ghost. The smell of cooling, breathing earth, the essence of the dusk, stole like a breeze into my brain. And as I lay, I looked and saw, pendent in the purple air, like a great yellow Indian topaz lost in an amethystine void, the digit of the moon, poised, as if on tiptoe, on the very rim of the brow of the

hill, whose sable edge it seemed to touch, with a fringe of soft and almost imperceptible iridescence, with magical contradiction, making the dark thing fair.

There the Great God stood, before me, with his Jewel on his brow.

And as I gazed, the moon stooped towards me, and whispered in my ear: Lo! I am the Star of Eve, the Diadem of Deity, the Planet of the Dusk, a holy Incarnation of loveliness beyond imagination. And thou, bathed in my beauty, drowned in my silver flood, softer than the glance cast by a mother on a fever-stricken child, wilt thou not worship and adore me, and own me for what I am, a deity indeed: Mistress of Herbs and Medicine of the soul: cool, pale, delicious, midnight Madonna, of all things dark and beautiful the darkest and the sweetest, and yet the fairest of the fair, Wilt thou not bow to me, as all men did of old, and as still do the peoples of the East, who set me as a moony tire in the tawny hair of the God of Gods, and hail me the imperial and only Jewel on the brow of this great dark world? Mystic Swan, sphere of crystal, camphor chalice, oozer of ambrosial ice, silent silver boat of heaven, by many names the ancients knew me, and did my godhead homage, calling me Artemis or Io, Bendis, Diana, Proserpine, Astarte, Atergatis or Isis, and a thousand other names, emblems all and symbols only of the Power which as Mother, Wife or Daughter draws, not drives, leading the whole creation willingly around its mystic dance: the power of attraction and affection which no man

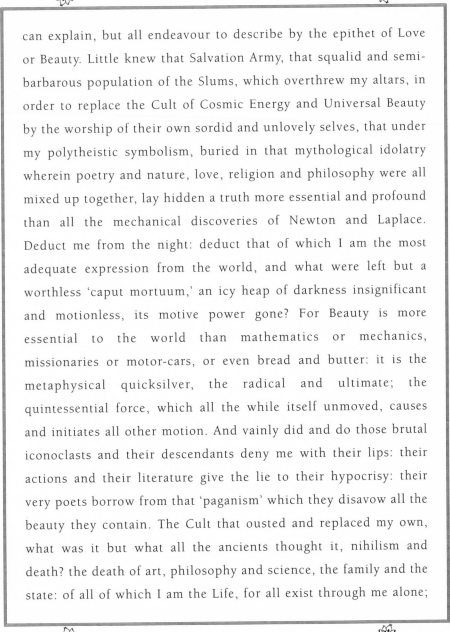

can explain, but all endeavour to describe by the epithet of Love or Beauty. Little knew that Salvation Army, that squalid and semi-barbarous population of the Slums, which overthrew my altars, in order to replace the Cult of Cosmic Energy and Universal Beauty by the worship of their own sordid and unlovely selves, that under my polytheistic symbolism, buried in that mythological idolatry wherein poetry and nature, love, religion and philosophy were all mixed up together, lay hidden a truth more essential and profound than all the mechanical discoveries of Newton and Laplace. Deduct me from the night: deduct that of which I am the most adequate expression from the world, and what were left but a worthless 'caput mortuum,' an icy heap of darkness insignificant and motionless, its motive power gone? For Beauty is more essential to the world than mathematics or mechanics, missionaries or motor-cars, or even bread and butter: it is the metaphysical quicksilver, the radical and ultimate; the quintessential force, which all the while itself unmoved, causes and initiates all other motion. And vainly did and do those brutal iconoclasts and their descendants deny me with their lips: their actions and their literature give the lie to their hypocrisy: their very poets borrow from that 'paganism' which they disavow all the beauty they contain. The Cult that ousted and replaced my own, what was it but what all the ancients thought it, nihilism and death? the death of art, philosophy and science, the family and the state: of all of which I am the Life, for all exist through me alone;

and all, in fact, returned in part, renascent after death, only when my altars had been once more erected, but under another name. For hypocrisy is the inevitable doom of all religion that denies me, since without me the world cannot get along. Yet all the time I continued and continue, circling in my cold inaccessible serenity around my unhappy sister Earth, not caring, like all true deities, whether there are any to see me and to worship me, or not. For it is the devotee who needs the deity, and not the deity the devotee. No true devotion asks for a return. For the one, it is sufficient to exist: Pure Being is enough: for the other is the passion and emotion, the imperfection, the struggle, ecstasy or despair. Absent, you wish for nothing but to see me: present, you burn with fierce desire to embrace me: mixed with my soul, you understand at last, that your thirst is one impossible to slake, for that by the very nature of your being, you are mocked. For Beauty, as my own old Indian sages understood, is as a Moon, inaccessible,[1] and as an Ocean, brine.[2] Those who strive to reach me, fail: those who drink me, maddened by the thirst for me, drink, not my beauty, which is Máyá, but its bitterness and salt....

And all at once, I felt something slip upon my knee. Two arms went round my neck, and a soft cheek was laid against my own. It was only my own little girl. And I said to her: Maya, do you know what the moon has been telling me about you? She says that you are a little idol, and a great humbug, and that you taste nasty and salt.

Durga
[2]láwanya

The child turned her face sharply round, without lifting it from mine, to see the moon, filling my eyes with her hair. So she lay, caressing my ear with her fairy fingers, symptom of profound meditation. And then she said: I do taste salt, when I have been crying. But how did the moon know? And why have I got salt water in me? Is it because I swallowed so much, when we bathed in the sea?

And I said: No, you didn't swallow enough, then. But long ago, once upon a time, you were a water baby, and so was the moon,

And I glanced, through the unceremonious hair, at Her Serene Highness; and I said softly: Mystic Lady, I know not which to call the true lunatics, the ancients who worshipped you, or the moderns, who do not. But you may count me, if you like, a believer and a worshipper, for the sake of this new young Isis or Aphrodite, this little Daughter of the Brine, upon my heart.

AN INCARNATION OF THE SNOW

SPIRITS OF THE SNOW

INVOCATION

'A Bow to the Flash of that Great Third Eye, which burned up the body of luckless Love, and doomed him, yearning for re-existence, to an endless chain of incarnations, as he springs again and again to life in the heart of youth or maid, suddenly catching sacred fire at the sight of the other sex.'

THERE is, in the northern quarter, a pinnacle of milk white snow, that shoots up into the eye of heaven like a sudden spout of leaping laughter,[1] saying as it were to the fleecy clouds that lazily float around it: Haha! my rivals, match my colour if you can. And near it, far below, lies a blue and silent lake, like a liquid lump of lapis-lazuli, whose swans, as they swim upon it, seem like pieces of the mountain mirrored in it, that have broken themselves off, and risen to the surface, to feed upon the tender stalks of the hosts of golden lotus-flowers that stud it like the stars of heaven, facing them right above.[2] And there, long ago, the Great God brought his new young bride, soon after they were married.[3]

So then, as that Lord of Creatures sported with the Daughter of the Mountain on the apex of that holy hill, it so fell out, by the decree of destiny, that they had a lovers' quarrel. For Maheshwara said to himself: What is sweeter than a lovers' quarrel? And what

[1] *Laughter, in Sanskrit poetry, is supposed to be coloured white.*
[2] *Lake Mánasa, like Mount Kailás, is in old Hindoo poetry always treated mythically. The curious can find, in the works of some modern travellers, prosaic accounts of the reality. But we should never visit holy places, if we wish to retain our faith.*
[3] *Those who wish for details as to this marriage in high life, can find them in that heavenly court circular, the 'Kumára Sambhava' of Kálidás; or go to Elephanta, with the book of Burgess in their hand.*

is the use of being a god, without superiority? Or shall it be supposed, that mortals have any sources of sweetness denied to us, their gods? Rather let us two lovers have a quarrel, sweeter than all the others exactly in proportion to our vast superiority: and, as it were, a type and model of all others, and yet containing a touch of ecstasy beyond them all.

So, therefore, as he suddenly stooped towards his wife, as if to kiss her, that crafty god allowed Gangá,[1] as if by accident, to peep out of his hair. And the Daughter of the Snowy Mountain saw her. And instantly, she bounded to her feet, and stood, turning from pale to red, and red to pale, and swelling with indignation, like a snake about to strike: looking, all the while, not at the god, but Gangá, and drawing herself, very slowly, up and back, till her two great rounded breasts seemed on the very point of parting in indignation from her body. And all at once, she cast upon the god a single glance of scorn and grief. And she left her place on Kailàs, and plunged, with a single swoop, like a falling star, down to the very margin of lake Mánasa, far, far away below; leaving that Mooncrested One all alone on the brow of the hill.

And then, the Lord of creatures animate and inanimate smiled softly to himself. And he said: Not without reason is my beloved called Chandi[2] in the world below. For the passion of her jealousy is, as it were, an index to the intensity of her love, and only its other side: and she resembles a flame, not only in its colour[3] but its heat. And so far, then, my little plot has succeeded, even

[1] *The river Ganges is fabled to have fallen from heaven and lost its way in the wilderness of the Great God's hair.*
[2] *Vixen*
[3] *Gauri, a common name of Párwatí, means 'pale red.'*

beyond my expectation, and now the quarrel I desired is skilfully set agoing.

And he looked away down to Mánasa, aiding the flight of his glance by the power of his mystical meditation.[1] And after a while, he said: Yonder she sits, grieving, like a female 'chakrawáka,' in the absence of her mate, on the very edge of the pool. And see, as she curves her slight and delicate figure in dejection, how exactly she resembles, at this distance, my digit of the moon, hanging low upon the sea, and reproduced, as she is, on the surface of the mere. Ha! did she only know it, she has very small reason to be jealous of no matter who it be. So ignorant is perfect beauty of its own irresistible fascination. And he looked at her awhile, with affection and delight. And after a while, he said: Come, now, let me carry out the remainder of my scheme. For it is not with me as with these poor mortals, who can only be in one place at a time. Now, then, I will be present with my angry beauty even in my absence, and under other forms, enjoy and feast at leisure and variety on the sweetness of her love-lorn sadness, and sip, like a bee, the nectar of my lotus, without her knowledge, and even against her will. So shall she, in her own despite, caress me unaware.

And instantly, that Master Yogi became invisible. And at that very moment, a wild swan shot down from Kailàs, towards the lake beneath: leaving that snowy peak with no companion but its own long dark blue shadow on the snow.

[1]*'The collyrium of Yoga': as if the magic was a sort of pomatum applied to the eye.*

THE KING'S AMOUR

THE KING'S AMOUR

CHAPTER I

UT in the meanwhile, that mountain-snow begotten lady sat melancholy by the lonely pool. And she sat on a slab of dark blue rock, that jutted over the water, bending a little backwards, leaning on her straight right arm, with the other laid upon her lap, and her two small feet crossed together, hanging over the lake, which lay absolutely still, as if it feared to lose, by untoward agitation, the images so beautifully painted on its glass. So as she drooped, with head a little on one side, and eyes fixed upon the water, a great bright tear stole slowly from under her long lashes, and hung for an instant on her cheek, before it fell into the pool.

And at that very moment, she heard, high up above her head, the scream of a wild swan. And she looked up, and saw him, as he shot like an arrow down into the water, and ran along its surface, throwing up, like a silver plough, a crystal spray, till at length he remained quiet on the bosom of the lake.

Then she called to the swan in his own language: O royal swan, come to me, and tell me the story of thy long journey. Whence hast thou come, and whither art thou bound? And hearing himself called, that noble swan came paddling rapidly towards her, with mighty strokes of his eager feet, that almost lifted him out of the

water. And Párwatí looked at him, with delight and admiration, mixed with sadness. And she said: Beautiful bird, how happy thou must be, oaring thy silver body like a boat through these cool waves, after thy long fatigue. Tell me thy story, and all that thou hast seen.

Then said the swan: O lady, I have come from a far off region, in the quarter of the South. And I travelled, never resting, over cities full of men, and over seas and deserts, that none pass over, save only the clouds, my fellows, and myself. And over moonlit mountains, where crystal fountains fall, plunging with deep murmur into gorges among the tops of trees: and over vast and sunny meadows, where multitudes of poppies and of lilies waved gently in the wind: yet never saw I anything so beautiful as this delicious pool, with thee upon its edge. Art thou a goddess, or one of the Widyádharís, or who? Then said Párwatí: O swan, I am the daughter of this snowy mountain, and my husband is the god that wears the moon in his hair.

And then, the swan rose erect in the water, and flapped his great white wings. And he exclaimed: Ha! Gaurí,[1] by thy favour I have woken from a dream. And recollection of my former birth has suddenly rushed into my soul, like a ray of light into the midst of utter darkness. And now I see, that anticipation of a future yet unknown may lurk in the living soul, like seed in soil, and grow up to maturity only in another life, when that one is extinct. For in my former birth, which has suddenly come back to me, know,

[1] *Pronounce the first syllable to rhyme with 'cow.'*

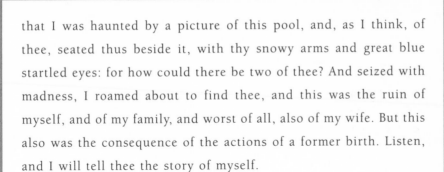

that I was haunted by a picture of this pool, and, as I think, of thee, seated thus beside it, with thy snowy arms and great blue startled eyes: for how could there be two of thee? And seized with madness, I roamed about to find thee, and this was the ruin of myself, and of my family, and worst of all, also of my wife. But this also was the consequence of the actions of a former birth. Listen, and I will tell thee the story of myself.

CHAPTER II

ND even as he spoke, suddenly there came a great black bee, which flew booming and grumbling round and round about the pool. And Párwatí said to the swan: Wait. And she called to the bee, which came at once, and settled on her hand. And he said: O Gaurí, for thou art surely she, I am very cold. For a strong wind caught me, as I was busy gathering honey on the hill, and blew me like a leaf high up into the air, till I lost my way among the icy clouds; and now I have arrived to die, frozen, by this cold pool. Then said the goddess: Nay, dear bee, it is not so. For I myself will warm thee, and when thou art recovered, I will show thee thy way to the warmer world below. And she took the bee, and put him in her bosom, saying: Sit thou there awhile, and listen in the meantime to the story of this royal swan.

So as she spoke, something touched her from above upon the hair. And she looked up quickly, and lo! there was a snake, hanging from the dead branch of a withered tree just over her head. And the snake said: O Gaurí, let me also listen to the story of the swan. For I also am cold, not, like this bee, with icy air, but fear. For Garud[1] saw me, as I crept through the jungle on the bank of Gangá, and he pounced upon me, and took me in his beak, intending to devour me at his leisure, and soared into the sky. And as luck would have it, as he drew near to the sun, he met his elder

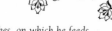

[1]*This Hindoo roc, the king of birds, is, or was, a deadly enemy of all snakes, on which he feeds.*

brother,[1] and entered into conversation with him. And in the course of conversation, he utterly forgot me, and let me go, and I dropped from his mouth and fell into this tree. And now I take refuge with thee. So the goddess put up her arm: and that snake let himself down, winding about her arm, till he reached her neck, and lay, circled about it like a necklace. And Párwatí said: Lie thou there, and become warm, and listen to the story of the swan. Yet beware, and do no injury to the bee that is reposing in my bosom, lest I curse thee, or send for Garud to devour thee.

So as she spoke, there came a bear, to drink at the pool. And as he drew near, he looked, and saw Párwatí and her companions. And he bowed before her. Then said the goddess: Bear, drink very quickly, and begone: for this swan is on the very point of telling me a story, and the noise of thy lapping will disturb us. Then said the bear: O Mother,[2] who wishes for water, when he can drench himself in the nectar of thy favour? Let me sit at thy feet, and be a footstool to thee, while the swan speaks, so that I also may listen. And he lay down at her feet, and Párwatí put her foot upon him, and the bear licked it with his tongue.

And then the goddess said: Now then, O swan, begin. So the swan came, and sat upon the water close beside her, and spoke, while she stroked his neck with one hand, making with the other a cover for the bee, with her foot upon the bear, and wearing the snake like a collar on her neck.

[1] *Aruna, the sun's charioteer.*
[2] *Amba, a name of Gauri.*

CHAPTER III

ND the swan said: O Gaurí, know, that in my former birth, I was the son of a king. And yet, well it would have been, had I been the son rather of the meanest fisherman; for then, it may be, I should not have sunk into this body of a swan. For kings resemble elephants, that go mad in the pride of their strength, and breaking loose from all restraint, commit appalling crimes, impossible of performance for creatures of a lower order. For my father had a queen for his wife, whom he loved to infatuation, so that whatever she might wish for, even in her sleep, he would use all his efforts to procure. Therefore she became like a spoiled child, and ran, as it were, riot in the garden of her wishes; and she went to the farther shore of the ocean of caprice and whim: asking for everything in the three worlds, and getting it at once. And at last, even to wait a very little while for no matter what it was became utterly intolerable to her. And little did my father think that he was with his own hand rooting up his race, and sowing the seed of its destruction, by feeding her desires till they turned to poison and produced at last an inexpiable crime. Ha! very wonderful is the blindness of lovers, ruining all by the very excess of their immoderate affection.

So then, after a while, the time came, when I was on the very point of being born. And then it was, that prompted no doubt by the influences of former crimes, and instigated by my father's

fatal indulgence, the queen my mother conceived an impious desire. And she said to my father: O son of a noble sire, I am seized with a frantic longing to bathe in a bath of human blood.[1] Cause it, therefore, quickly to be prepared. Then even my father was struck with horror. And he exclaimed: Fie! fie! Out on such a hideous desire! And instantly my mother fell into a passion of tears. And she said: I will positively have my bath. Know that it is either that, or thou art guilty of my death, and that of thy son, now actually knocking at the door of life. Answer it to thy ancestors. Then my father went away in great perplexity. And he said to himself: Either way I shall be guilty of destroying life: and now, then, which guilt is the lesser? For I do not doubt, that if she does not get her way, she will destroy both herself and the child. Therefore, after a while, he determined that the least evil would be, to comply with her desire; blinded by the threefold mist of his evil destiny, his love for her, and his own longing for a son.

So he sent for his chief huntsman, and his commander-in-chief. And when they came, he said to them: Go out now into the forest, and catch me, very quickly, a hundred Bhils, or Shabaras, and bring them back alive. And if you do not return within the setting of another sun, your own heads will be the penalty.

So those two officers went out, hunting that very strange game; and the next day they returned, joyfully, bringing with them a century of very miserable Bhils. And then the King sent for his

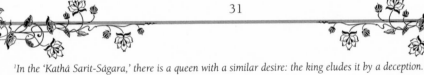

[1] *In the 'Kathá Sarit-Ságara,' there is a queen with a similar desire: the king eludes it by a deception.*

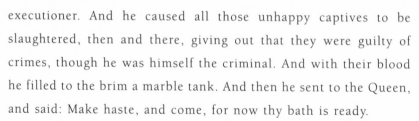

executioner. And he caused all those unhappy captives to be slaughtered, then and there, giving out that they were guilty of crimes, though he was himself the criminal. And with their blood he filled to the brim a marble tank. And then he sent to the Queen, and said: Make haste, and come, for now thy bath is ready.

And the Queen, excited and overjoyed by reason of the gratification of her desire, made great haste, and hurried to that unholy tank. But no sooner had she set eyes on it, than she was seized with such a horror, that every hair upon her body suddenly stood erect. And she stood there, for a single instant, trembling all over, like a bamboo shivering in an icy breeze, rooted, as it were, to the ground. And all at once, she turned away, as if to flee: and she uttered a terrible shriek, and fell to earth in a swoon. And at that very moment, I was born.

– Ha! Gaurí, art thou attentive? And the goddess answered: Dear Swan, speak on: I listen. And she caressed his snowy neck with the lotus of her hand.

CHAPTER IV

O then, as soon as I came into the world, the King my father went wild with joy, and all his kingdom with him. And I grew up with the eyes of my father and mother fastened as it were upon me, for I was their only child. And they looked upon me as the fruit of their birth, feasting on me with insatiable delight, so much so, that they clean forgot the evil deed that had heralded my coming, putting it away like something ended, and altogether past and gone; not knowing, O daughter of Himálaya, that actions are the tree, and good or evil fortune the inevitable fruit, which no oblivion can cheat, nor stratagem avert. But in the meantime, while the nemesis of their crime was slowly ripening in the darkness, I lived, the focus of all their attention: and the world was ransacked, to adorn me, and my mother made me the very centre of all her wishes, and my parents passed their time like children, of whom I was the toy.

So then, one day, as they sat together, rejoicing in me as I played before them, a child of seven years, there came in all at once a chamberlain. And he said: O Maháraj, there stands without, at the palace gate, an old Bhikshu,[1] a very incarnation of the evening of life; and he sent me to thee, saying: Go quickly, and bid the King come out to me at once, and bring his child with him. And I pray the King to show mercy.[2] And hearing this, my father was very angry. And he exclaimed: What! am I become the slave of an old

[1] *A holy beggar, generally a Buddhist.*
[2] *To himself, that is, for bringing such a peremptory order.*

mendicant? Go, and tell him to be off, rejoicing that his age protects him. But my mother said: Nay, be not hasty: do nothing rashly: for who knows? For what old mendicant would dare to send the King such a message, unless he was something more? For often it has come about that deities have come disguised to the doors of kings. Moreover, if he should be irritated, he might possibly curse the child: whereas, as it is, doubtless he has come to bless him. So what harm is there in this? Do thou rather be advised by me, and take the child, and go and see this old Bhikshu, as he wishes. For the power of asceticism is more than even that of kings.

So my father, persuaded by her, here as always, took me up in his arms. And together we went out, not knowing that we had looked upon her for the last time. And when we went down, and reached the palace gate, lo! there stood an old beggar, in a yellow garment, with a head as bare as a copper pot, and a face like the skin of a withered mango, and eyes like a steady flame. And as soon as we stood before him, that old mendicant said slowly: O King, how is this? Thy child is covered with blood. And I shrank from that strange old man, not knowing what he meant; for then I had not heard, as afterwards I learned too well, the story of my birth. And I looked at my father as I clung to him, and lo! he also was abashed, and he also seemed to me to shrink. Then said the old mendicant: O King, good shall come only to him that doeth good; but evil follows evil, as thy shadow follows thee. And now,

this child lives, and yet shall live, in the shadow of a crime that stained him at his birth with blood: but as for the criminals, their punishment is close at hand. As they dipped their souls in guilt by hankering after things forbidden, so shall he, by hereditary transmission,[1] long for what shall steal away his memory and his reason, and make him, whether he will or no, the destruction of his family, till he fall into a lower birth. Aye! thou who wouldst fain forget, didst thou imagine thou couldst escape the ripening of the fruit of the creeper of crime? And then, that ill-boding old mendicant turned, and went slowly along the road, until he disappeared. But my father stood silent, like a picture painted on a wall, gazing after him as he went, while I clung to him in terror. And so as we stood together, suddenly there arose a hubbub, and a cry, and wailing in the palace behind us. And all at once, all the servants ran out in a crowd together, and stood around us, exclaiming: Alas! the Queen! alas! the Queen! Then said my father: What is the matter? And as he spoke, I felt his grasp tighten, as he held my shoulder, till I almost screamed with pain. And a female doorkeeper stood forward, and said: O Maháraj, the Queen has fallen from a high window, and broken herself to pieces on the ground below. For in her curiosity to see for herself, from the women's apartments, what you were doing with the old mendicant, she leaned out till she lost her balance, and tumbled down, and now she is dead.

So when my father heard this, he let me go, and stood a long

---

[1] *This is one of those points at which the old Indian theory of metempsychosis fits exactly in with modern scientific ideas: a coincidence so much admired by Schopenhauer, who must have been a Hindoo sage in a former birth.*

while, without speaking; and his head hung down upon his breast. And at the last, he said aloud, very slowly, speaking to himself: I was the guilty culprit, and yet now, she has suffered, and I am the murderer of my own wife. And she would have followed me: therefore now, I must follow her. Or shall it be said, in my dominions, that all who murdered their wives were punished with death, except the King? And he took his dagger out of his belt. And he exclaimed: Lo! ye of my household: ye are all my witnesses, that I leave this son of mine as a deposit in the hands of my brother. And he put the knife to his throat, and ran it through with a firm hand, till the point stood out behind, and then fell to the ground, and lay in a pool of his own blood.

So I became an orphan, and that terrible old mendicant, a speaker of the truth.

– Ha! Girijá,[1] art thou attentive? And the goddess answered: Dear Swan, speak on: I listen. And she caressed his neck with the lotus of her hand.

[1] i.e. 'born of the mountain,' – an epithet of Párwatí.

CHAPTER V

THEN they sent hastily for my uncle, bidding him come and take charge of the kingdom and of me. And when he arrived, he burned with all the customary rites the bodies of my two parents; and he sent messengers in all directions to discover the old mendicant whose words had been the immediate occasion[1] of their death: but never found so much as his shadow. And thereafter he remained, preserving me as a deposit committed to the hands of a faithful guardian, and administering for me the affairs of my widowed kingdom, till I should become of age to bear the weight of it myself. And I, in the meanwhile, grew gradually up to manhood, and in course of time I learned from others the story of my parents' crime. For their death had made it a byword and a wonder in the world. And the meeting with the old mendicant remained fixed like an indelible picture stamped upon my mind, hanging before my eyes constantly like a curtain, concealing what I burned to know, until I found it out. And I became myself an object of extreme curiosity to all, and the people looked upon me with anxiety, mixed with admiration, knowing my story, and wondering what would happen next. For I was the very image of my father, who was the handsomest man in all his dominions; and yet the Creator, when he reproduced in my instance my father's body, had placed within it my mother's soul. For I was haunted by strange desires, and tenanted, as it were, by

[1]*'Nimitta': a word which combines the senses of 'causing' and 'prognosticating.'*

the demon of a burning thirst for something I knew not what; and I resembled an incarnation of excessive longing, passionately striving and straining in the darkness towards an object that it cannot see. And never being able to attain to my desire, or even comprehend it and discover what it was that I desired, I became the prey of melancholy, and I shrank from the society of men, nursing and feeding my blind appetite in secret, and above all fearful, lest any other person should discover what I did not even know myself. And I loved to wander, utterly alone, in the forest, or to ramble in the hills, giving out that I was hunting, as indeed I was, after a fashion of my own. And dismissing my attendants, I used to roam, by night and day, listening to the sound of the wind as it played in the trees, and gazing into the distance, with tears in my eyes, I knew not why. And often I went stealthily, stealing on tiptoe among the trees, and passing noiselessly from trunk to trunk, as if I feared lest the rustle of a leaf should scare away the thing I sought, though what it was I could not tell. And often I lay still for hours, striving to guess my own secret, and racking my imagination for an answer that never came. So I continued to live, more resembling one dreaming than a waking man, suspended continually between despair and expectation, and as it were starting at every noise, and constantly looking as it were behind me, as if my secret were my own shadow.

And in the meanwhile, my uncle, steadfast in his duty, and anxious for the family, strove to get me married; but in vain. For

all the neighbouring kings, and everybody else, knew my story, and looked upon me as one lying under a curse, whose family was doomed: and there was not one of them who would have given me so much as a hair of his daughter's head, though I had offered him my kingdom in exchange. And this state of affairs, like the circle produced on water by the dropping of a stone, spread ever wider and wider: till not only in my own domains, but in every quarter of the world, no man even of the lowest caste but would have deemed himself dishonoured by the very suspicion that he was willing to give me his daughter as a wife. So the door of marriage seemed to be shut, as it were, in my face, and I was known through the world as the Bachelor[1] King.

And at last, my uncle gave up the idea of my marriage in despair, saying: Thou must find, if thou canst, something to marry other than a woman: for the women will not have thee. And now, unless some goddess or demon takes pity on thee, thou art certainly doomed. But I laughed within myself, caring no more for my disaster than do the forest elephants for the touch of the creepers that whip them as they push through the forest heart, And I said to my uncle: O uncle, why not endeavour to buy for me a wife, if all other methods fail? Or dost thou fear to find that, in so bad a market, the very merchants will not sell?

– Ha! Durgá,[2] art thou attentive? And the goddess answered: Dear Swan, speak on: I listen, And she caressed his snowy neck with the lotus of her hand.

[1]An ironical term – ' brahmachári' –, as though to say, 'one who does not wish for a wife,' though, in fact, he could not get one.
[2]The 'inaccessible' one: a name of Párwatí.

CHAPTER VI

O then, it happened, that at length my uncle went himself, after my parents, along the Great Road: and I succeeded to the throne, wifeless as I was. And my uncle said to me, upon his deathbed: How shall I meet thy parents, after whom I am going, or what shall I answer, when they say to me: Hast thou married our son? So he died, grieving that he left me unmarried; and yet he was hardly dead before my wife appeared, as though she had only waited to appear, until he died: or as if he had himself gone to fetch her from the other world.

For soon after he was gone, it happened, that one day I went out into the forest, giving out that I was going on a hunting expedition. And after travelling for many days, suddenly I seized my opportunity, and giving all my retinue the slip, I escaped, and plunged alone into the thickest of the wood. And I wandered about, buried in my dreams, till suddenly I found, exactly in front of me, a wall. And I examined it, mounting a tree that grew beside it, and within it was a hermitage. So I climbed like a thief over the wall, and entered stealthily its holy precinct.

And there I found myself in a glade, studded with colossal trees, banyans and sacred pippals, whose ascending and descending roots and branches wound and twisted about each other with affection, like limbs of human bodies,[1] as if they were the dwellings of the souls of former saints come to guard that holy

---

[1] *What a pity that poor Ovid never was in India! He might have seen, by every roadside, his metamorphoses of women into trees realised before his eyes.*

shrine, and sanctify the sap within their bark. And all round them, in their shade, were browsing innumerable deer, which raised their heads to look at me, unstartled, since every form of fear was banished from that secluded pale. And I saw, in the distance, the thin blue lines of sacrificial smoke rising from their fires, like prayers visible to the eye,[1] straight up into the air, as though to say, from this exact spot is the shortest way to heaven. And near me was a smooth black pool, strewn with great white lotus flowers, beside which, on the edge, great cranes were sitting motionless in rows, like meditating 'munis'; and a little way behind them were other rows of jars, left there beyond a doubt by the daughters of the hermits after watering their flowers, not more motionless than the birds. And seized with rapture at the contemplation of the stillness and quiet of that hallowed place of refuge, I lay down, hidden in the foliage, to rest; and as I listened to the water dropping from a fountain somewhere concealed among the trees, unawares I fell asleep.

And, after a while, the sound of voices woke me. And I looked up, and peered through the foliage that concealed me, and saw, a little way off, a knot of young women coming rapidly towards me, talking as they came among themselves, and laughing. And I also laughed to myself, and lay still, saying to myself: Did these very pretty daughters of the hermits only know, who it was so close beside them, they would flee like yonder deer before a wolf! And I watched them with curiosity as they

[1] *How prayers ascended to heaven, was a question which much exercised the mind of Sir Isaac Newton, who brought them into line with his corpuscular theory of light, by supposing them to ascend in a sort of atomic smoke. He would, no doubt, have been much pleased to find his view reflected in old Hindoo poetry.*

came, wondering with what object they were coming: for they moved quickly, crowding about someone in the midst of them, and all chattering at once. So then, one who was their leader, suddenly exclaimed: Here we are, and this is the image of the god. And I looked, and saw, seated in the hollow of an old banyan tree, a vermilion stained image of the Elephant-faced deity,[1] close beside me. And the speaker said again: Now, then, let us all return, leaving only Kuwalayinî[2] alone with the god. Perhaps he will reveal some cure for her disease. Then said another: Let her pray for a husband: he is the true elixir: and who ever obtained a husband without praying to Ganapati? And I heard, out of the midst of them, a voice like a 'kokila,' saying: Nay, do not leave me all alone. Then said another: Ha! Ha! dost thou imagine that the Tusky One will turn one of these trees into a husband for thee? There is nothing to be feared. And suddenly they all ran away, like a flock of pigeons or parrots taking flight, leaving one only standing still, in front of the image of the god in the tree.

So as she stood, I watched her, as little aware of what was in her heart, as was she of who was just beside her. And she waited, standing absolutely still, watching her companions disappear. And then she turned, and cast a glance at the god in the tree: and she looked round, as if apprehensive lest someone other than the god should overhear her. And all unconscious, she looked straight at me, and I saw her for the first time. And at that moment, another god saw his opportunity, and entered my heart, through the

[1]*The god of good luck – Ganesha.*
[2]*'A pool of lotuses.*

loophole of my eyes. And certainly he never had a weapon more pointed or more poisonous than the one who stood before me. For she was nearly as tall as I was myself; and I think that the Creator must have made her to show how straight a thing could be compounded of a multitude of intoxicating curves. For she looked as slender as the stalk of a sugar-cane: and yet her shoulders and her arms and her bosom and her hips were deep and full and glorious and heavy; and as she stood resting on one small foot, with the other knee a little bent, raising both her arms for a moment to touch with her fingers the mass of dark hair knotted on the top of her head, which she turned a very little as if on purpose to exhibit the incomparable poise and balance of her neck, she resembled a great jar, moulded by the celestial Potter as a receptacle for the nectar churned from ocean, or a vessel destined to catch the midnight ooze dripped from the moonstones hanging on some terrace in the elysium of Alaka.

And as I gazed at her, bewildered by her beauty, all at once, like one recollecting something he has forgotten, I started, and I said to myself: Can it be, that I have stumbled accidentally on the very thing for which I have been looking all my life? Or if not all, then at any rate, part of it, in this delicious woman's form? For I seem, somehow, as it were, to recognise and recollect her, though beyond all doubt, I never saw her anywhere before. For who that had ever seen her, even for an instant, would ever be able to forget her again? – Ha! Gaurí, very blind are mortals to their

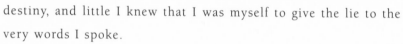

destiny, and little I knew that I was myself to give the lie to the very words I spoke.

So as she looked, with huge sad eyes, full at me, without seeing, revolving something in her mind, I began to tremble like a leaf, unable to endure them: and at that very moment, she smiled a very little to herself, with a smile that caught me like a fly in the mesh of its sweet. And she turned towards the god, and stretched out her arms towards him, and said, in a low voice: O Rider on the Mouse, these silly girls, my dear companions, speak idly, without thinking, or knowing what they say: and yet they resemble archers that hit a mark at which they did not aim: and all unaware, they have touched the very heart of my disease. Yet how can they, who never felt it, understand the pain, which Love inflicts upon his hopeless victims? And who was ever more hopeless than myself, or what maiden's desire was ever fixed upon an object so distant and inaccessible as mine? And therefore it is, my heart and my feet are heavy, and the weight of my body seems to weigh me to the ground. And sleep has forsaken me, and I am become, as it were, tinder and fuel for the flame that ever burns me. My sole refuge is in thy favour. As I have meditated on the sole of thy foot night and day, do thou requite me in kind, and intercede for me with the deity of the flowery bow, and beg of him a boon.

And she stopped short, and faltered, and hesitated, while a deep red blush suddenly started and ran like a conflagration over her face. And she murmured, as though to whisper in the very ear of the god: Make me, O Subduer of even the most terrific Obstacles,[1] the wife of the King that has no wife; and give him to me for a husband. And he shall bless thee as well as I, for there is no one to pity him in the three worlds, except myself.

And as the words left her lips, she turned instantly deadly pale. But I started, struck by the thunderbolt of astonishment. And instantly, delight and passion poured into my soul like a wave of the sea, and almost broke my heart. And I said to myself: Ha! so this child of beauty had pity for me that no one else had. Ha! little I thought to find myself shrined in the heart of a hermit's daughter. And instantly I left my covert. And I exclaimed: O maiden, thou art surely the favourite of the elephant-god: for here I am in person, the very answer to thy prayer.

– Ha! Bhagawatí,[2] art thou attentive? And the goddess answered: Dear Swan, speak on: I listen. And she caressed his snowy neck with the lotus of her hand.

[1] 'Wignajit,' the 'vanquisher of obstacles,' is a name of Ganesha.
[2] 'Holy One': a name of Párwatí.

CHAPTER VII

ND then, that dark-haired beauty stood for a moment, staring at me with round bewildered lotus eyes, in which shame was mixed with terror and the extremity of wonder, to see her wish granted so unexpectedly as soon as uttered: and then she suddenly swayed, and sank to earth, bereft of sense. But I leaped towards her, and caught her, and received in strong arms the bride given me by herself and the god. And I looked towards him, as he watched us, saying: O god of good luck, surely thy power must be very great, that can so easily bring about things apparently impossible. For what could possibly be more unlikely than that I should have come here as I did, for her to find me in the bushes in the very nick of time? And I said to my wife, as she lay swooning in my arms: Dear, though thou hast. like an 'abhisáriká,' given thyself to me of thy own accord, I will not abuse thy confidence, nor take an unfair advantage, though I would give my soul to kiss thee, all marble white and lifeless as thou art, on those delicious lips. And then, I shouted aloud, saying to myself: Doubtless her companions cannot be very far.

And hearing the shout, all the deer suddenly stopped grazing, and looked at me reproachfully: and in a little while, that band of maidens also reappeared. And seeing me standing, with their companion in my arms, they also stopped short, as they ran

towards us, and stood, exactly like the deer whose eyes their own resembled, balanced in the swing of irresolution, half terrified of me, half drawn towards me by curiosity and astonishment. And, seeing them at a stand, I called out: O timid beauties, do not fear: for I am one, rather to protect you than molest you. Come quickly and render assistance to this lovely playfellow of yours, who has suddenly swooned away at the sight of me, as well indeed she might. Then they came forward, collecting courage, with hesitation. And one, speaking for all the others, said politely: Sir, who art thou, and what is thy name and family, and how in the world hast thou suddenly appeared in this our hermitage, in which nothing ever comes but the hermits and their families?

And I said laughing: O fair one, I am only the husband of this sister of thine, whom Ganapati has sent her in answer to her prayer. Take her, and restore her to life, of which for the moment astonishment has deprived her: and she will herself tell thee all about it.

Then those maidens busied themselves about her, whispering to each other, and stealing at me glances out of the corners of their eyes. And I said to them: Where shall I find her parents, or her guardians? For since the god has given her to me, I must go and ask for her in proper form. Then they said: Sir, she has no parents, being an orphan under the protection of the sage. And I said: Take me, then, into the presence of the sage.

Then some of them led me away to a pool, near which that old sage was seated, buried in meditation. And when he came to himself, I bowed before him, and told him who I was, and explained to him the state of the case, and asked him for his ward. Then that old man said slowly: Take her: she is thine. For all this tallies exactly with a dream which I had concerning her: and beyond a doubt, that Remover of Difficulties would never have dropped thee, as it were, from the sky, so strangely and so abruptly into her mouth, had it not been his express intention to unite you. And what the deity desires, let us not oppose, for he is wise.[1] And yet, O King, many times in this lower world have mortals, blinded by their fate, asked for something, and rejoiced to obtain it, which, could they have foreseen the future, they would have striven at all costs or hazards to avoid: and it may be, that both this maiden and thyself are instances in point.

So that old sage spoke, as if to warn me of the future; gifted, by reason of his austerities, with insight and prophetic skill. But I disregarded it, putting his words, like wind, aside, as prompted by the natural despondency of age. And I said: O father, I accept thy gift, and venerate thy wisdom. But as for the future, who can tell, or who can escape the destiny that is written on his brow?

Then said that old far-seeing sage: Happy the wife that her lord remembers: but alas for the wife that her lord forgets!

– Ha! Satí,[2] art thou attentive? And the goddess answered: Dear Swan, speak on: I listen. And she caressed his snowy neck with the lotus of her hand.

48

[1]*Ganapati is the god of wisdom.*
[2]*'The Pure One': a name of Párwatí.*

CHAPTER VIII

THEN I took leave of the sage, and went and found my followers, and returned very quickly to my capital: and I came again, and fetched my bride, and married her with all the ceremonies. But my subjects were so astounded, to see that I had somehow or other managed to find, after all, a wife, that torn as it were asunder by amazement and rejoicing, they almost lost their reason. And the women, in their vexation, almost abandoned the body, exclaiming: Who is this courageous beauty, who has actually dared to marry one whom we all despised? And they all waited, as if expecting something doomed to come about.

But in the meanwhile I, having found a wife in spite of them, proceeded now to live with her. And she, for her part, loved me better than ever Rati[1] did her lord, making of me her deity, and as it were, breathing only by my permission, and existing only for my delight. And yet, O Gaurí, I requited her not in kind. For I loved her, it is true, with passion, and exceedingly, and yet, strange! with a love, in which, I know not how, there seemed always to be one thing wanting: and my devotion to her resembled a pool, in which the lotus that completes and makes it perfect, was not there. And this was my own fault, and due to my insatiable desire for something further, whose nature I could not tell. For I was haunted continually by the feeling that I had made a mistake, in

[1] *Wife of the god of love.*

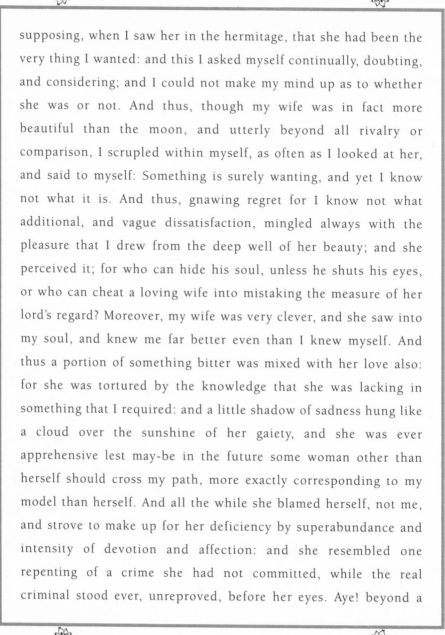

supposing, when I saw her in the hermitage, that she had been the very thing I wanted: and this I asked myself continually, doubting, and considering; and I could not make my mind up as to whether she was or not. And thus, though my wife was in fact more beautiful than the moon, and utterly beyond all rivalry or comparison, I scrupled within myself, as often as I looked at her, and said to myself: Something is surely wanting, and yet I know not what it is. And thus, gnawing regret for I know not what additional, and vague dissatisfaction, mingled always with the pleasure that I drew from the deep well of her beauty; and she perceived it; for who can hide his soul, unless he shuts his eyes, or who can cheat a loving wife into mistaking the measure of her lord's regard? Moreover, my wife was very clever, and she saw into my soul, and knew me far better even than I knew myself. And thus a portion of something bitter was mixed with her love also: for she was tortured by the knowledge that she was lacking in something that I required: and a little shadow of sadness hung like a cloud over the sunshine of her gaiety, and she was ever apprehensive lest may-be in the future some woman other than herself should cross my path, more exactly corresponding to my model than herself. And all the while she blamed herself, not me, and strove to make up for her deficiency by superabundance and intensity of devotion and affection: and she resembled one repenting of a crime she had not committed, while the real criminal stood ever, unreproved, before her eyes. Aye! beyond a

doubt, some crime she had committed in a previous existence must have been the reason why she was joined by the deity to such a husband as myself. Or was it but a prank, played by the roguish god of love, merely for his own amusement? for certainly he loves to fill the heart with passion for an object all unworthy of its esteem. Nor was there a living man except myself, who could have found in my wife were it only the shadow of a defect. But I was only the instrument of my own punishment, doomed to self-originated misery, by reason of my parents' crime.

So, then, we lived together, enjoying a happiness that was spotted, like a panther's skin, by the discontent arising from my own imagination. And I continued wearing, like Wishnu, on my breast, a 'Koustubha'[1] of which I did not know the value, until in my infatuation I had broken it to pieces with my own hands, throwing away my Shrí.[2] And then at last there came about a thing, which though but itself a drop, filled up the cup of my wife's uneasiness, and was, as it were, the precursor of the end.

For one day, as I was roaming at sunset in the forest with my wife, we saw, coming along towards us, an old ascetic. And as he drew near, and we were on the very point of bowing to his merit, suddenly that holy old man placed his bare foot exactly on a blade of withered grass, which ran into it like a thorny needle, and injured him. And instantly, that exasperated old man uttered a loud yell, and began to hop, nursing his foot; and all at once he threw himself upon his knees, and began to dig and grub at the

[1] *The great jewel, so named, worn by Wishnu.*
[2] *The goddess Shrí is Wishnu's wife: and the word also means prosperity, good fortune, brightness.*

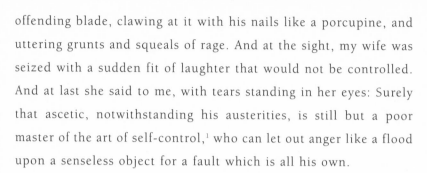

offending blade, clawing at it with his nails like a porcupine, and uttering grunts and squeals of rage. And at the sight, my wife was seized with a sudden fit of laughter that would not be controlled. And at last she said to me, with tears standing in her eyes: Surely that ascetic, notwithstanding his austerities, is still but a poor master of the art of self-control,[1] who can let out anger like a flood upon a senseless object for a fault which is all his own.

Then that acrimonious old sage looked at her grimly. And he said: O hilarious ill-mannered beauty, that scoffest at my merit in thy ignorance, not having perceived, as I did, the demon that had entered the blade with the express purpose of so injuring my foot as to prevent me from continuing my pilgrimage to the sacred bathing places, know, that thou art thyself on the very eve of suffering, like this grass, for a fault not thy own, as do all the creatures, animate or inanimate, of this lower world, involved as they are in the network of criminality. And very soon indeed thy own self control will be tried in the hottest fire; and then thou wilt recollect thy present laughter, and repent it, and atone for it with tears. For learn, that thou hast laughed for the last time in thy life.

And instantly, my wife's laughter vanished, like a flame suddenly extinguished. And she said: Reverend Sir, I am rightly reproved by thee, and my laughter, though involuntary, was altogether without excuse. And I looked at her, and said within myself: Now the old 'muní' will undoubtedly be mollified, for even a stone would be moved by the beauty of her submission. But that cantankerous old

---

[1] *Because to 'master the self,' 'overcome the ego,' is the very essence and aim of asceticism: and 'jitátmá,' the name of a true ascetic, means one who has done it.*

man would not be appeased. And turning his back upon her, he went away, muttering and limping. And I said to her: No matter: let this old incarnation of ill-humour go, to accumulate merit[1] where he will, forgotten. But my wife was like one seized with sudden melancholy, as if that old man's words had cursed her, casting over her a spell.

– Ha! Kálí,[2] art thou attentive? And the goddess answered: Dear Swan, speak on: I listen. And she caressed his snowy neck with the lotus of her hand.

CHAPTER IX

ND then, almost immediately afterwards, that came about which she foresaw and feared. For one day it happened, that as I sat by my palace window, I heard in the street a noise. And I listened, and lo! it became a hubbub, and then a roar: so that finally I said to myself: Doubtless something unusual is going on in the city. And curious to know what in the world could be the matter, I sent a chamberlain to see. So then, after a while, that chamberlain returned. And he said, with excitement: O Maháraj, this is a very strange affair, the like of which, as I imagine, has never occurred before, either in this city of ours or any other. For I learn by enquiry, that there came into the city, a day or two ago, an old mime, from nobody knows where. But the people say, that he must

[1]*The virtue of an ascetic was regarded as a sort of actual lump or store of valuable material, a bank of good works, added together grain by grain, ensuring an equivalent reward.*
[2]*'Black,' a name of Párwatí – cp. the black Virgin, black Osiris, &c.*

be a Yaksha, or a Pishácha, or a Rákshasa, or it may be, some Kinnara or Gandharwa, banished by reason of a curse from his home in the Snowy Mountain; since he has a face like a horse, and is clothed as nobody else was ever clothed before, and carries about with him a long flute, like the enemy of Kans.[1] And he goes through the city from house to house, dancing and singing and playing and telling stories: and all those who listen to his songs are driven mad: so that by means of them he has set the whole city in an uproar. And now the citizens have collected in a body, and seized him, and at this very moment they are carrying him away outside the city, to offer him up a sacrifice to Durgá, as is suitable. For his songs have set wives against their husbands and husbands against their wives, and caused many of the citizens to abandon their trades and their families, and even their bodies, in disgust. For he plays not so much upon his pipe as upon every man's heart, telling each one of something far better than he has got, and inflaming him with the fire of discontent and a raging thirst for pictures in the sky, so that he utterly despises his lot and everything about him. And as I said, some, out of extreme abomination, and a kind of ecstasy, have already abandoned the body of their own accord; and beyond a doubt, if he remained alive, gradually all thy subjects would follow their example, till none were left at all. But by this time, he will have paid the penalty of his crimes, and answered for them with his life.

And instantly, I started from my seat. And I shouted: Run! run!

[1]*Krishna: the flute player par excellence. The Gandharwas and Kinnaras were the heavenly musicians with horses' heads. This last peculiarity does not seem easy of explanation.*

Away! fly! pursue this criminal, and save him, and bring him here, alive and uninjured, or thy own life shall be the forfeit. And as I spoke, I looked, and lo! my wife was standing, gazing at me, pale as snow, with terror in her eyes. And she stretched out both hands towards me, murmuring: See him not, see him not. And I said quickly: O fearful one, of what art thou afraid? And as I did so, the chamberlain disappeared, like an arrow shot out of a bow: and immediately I heard a tumult in the palace, and the galloping of horses in the street. And I waited, walking up and down, listening, with a soul as it were on tiptoe, so great was my anxiety to see this miserable mime brought back alive. And I muttered to myself: Ha! who knows what I may learn from this fellow, coming, as it seems, from the ends of the earth? And at the very thought of him, all my old longing suddenly revived within me, and my soul began to burn with the fire of anticipated delight: and all at once, I caught sight of my wife's eyes, fixed upon me, as I wandered up and down, like nails.

And I started, as I saw them, for they resembled the eyes of one gazing at his own death coming straight towards him. And I stopped short, and stood, looking at her; and as I did so, she came quickly up to me, and said with emotion: O think again, before it is too late. Send away this old musician, unhurt by all means, if thou wilt, but above all, unseen, unheard, by thee.

And I answered her roughly, for my heart smote me, within: and I knew that she was right, and that whatever might befall, she had

good cause to reproach me, and to fear for herself. For my anxiety to see him was, as it were, infidelity to her in another shape. And feeling that she fathomed my very soul, I said with anger: O Kuwalayiní, what is this? Art thou then so jealous, even of my ears, that I must not even so much as listen to the music of an old itinerant mime, lest he should tell me a story of some other woman than thyself?

And instantly, she shrank, as if my words had been a blow. And a shadow settled down upon her face, which changed, and lost its colour and expression, till it looked like a mask: and at that very moment, there was heard a bustle in the palace; and immediately, the chamberlain returned. And he said joyfully: Long-lived one, we are here, having snatched that melancholy mountebank from the very jaws of death: and we placed him upon a horse, and brought him hither like the wind: and now he is outside, waiting only for your order to admit him.

And I said: Bring him in. So they went out, to fetch him. But my wife stood gazing at the door, like an incarnation of despair.

– Ha! Kanyá,[1] art thou attentive? And the goddess answered: Dear Swan, speak on: I listen. And she caressed his snowy neck with the lotus of her hand.

---

[1] *'Maiden': a name of Párwatí – cp. 'Koré.'*

CHAPTER X

ND then, the mime entered, and stood at last on the marble floor before me. And I gazed upon him, and at the very sight of him, I became instantly lost in wonder, so that I utterly forgot my wife. And I said within myself: Surely the Creator framed him in a moment of singularity, and as if wishing to exhibit skill in the manufacture of the grotesque. Or can it be, that he is really one of a class, and that there actually is another being like him anywhere in the three worlds? For tall though he was, he stooped, with high and rounded shoulders, till he resembled a crane, with long thin arms and legs that were altogether bare; for he wore as his only garment as it were a bodice of red bark, that fitted him like a skin, covering, like the shell of a tortoise, nothing but his trunk. And as my chamberlain had said, his face was like a horse's face, extraordinarily long, and his two large eyes were set in it at a distance from each other and his mouth, and were full of timidity and distrust. And two enormous ears, fleshy and with hairy tips, resembling those of a cow, stuck straight out from his head, around which fell like a mane a bushy mass of coarse straight hair: and his lips twitched continually, as if they were alive. And round his neck hung by a string a long bamboo cane, pierced with innumerable holes, which he never ceased to feel at with fingers that were knotted like the joints of the pipe on which they played.

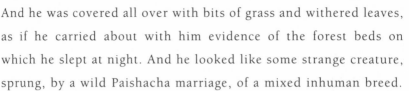

And he was covered all over with bits of grass and withered leaves, as if he carried about with him evidence of the forest beds on which he slept at night. And he looked like some strange creature, sprung, by a wild Paishacha marriage, of a mixed inhuman breed.

And after a while, I said: What kind of man art thou, if indeed thou art a man at all: and whence hast thou come, to breed mischief in my city? But he made no answer. Then I said again: Is it fear that keeps thee silent, robbing thee of thy faculty of speech, and seeming to fill thy eyes, as well indeed it might, seeing that by my orders thou hast just been snatched from the mouth of death? And still he made no answer: looking at me all the while with shifty eyes and lips that seemed to mock me, being always as it were on the very verge of utterance that never came, and fumbling and feeling with his fingers at his pipe. And at last I said with irritation: Play, then, if thou canst not speak, and give me a specimen of that skill of thine, which drives my people mad,

And then, all at once, that lean old mime made a stride towards me, so sudden and so eager, that I started against my will. And he put, like a flash of lightning, his long pipe to his lips, bending forward as he did so, and fixing his large eyes on mine: and yet they seemed to look, not at me, but at something far away behind him. And as I listened, all at once, there came from that pipe a strange sound, resembling the low muttering of many voices, and the rustling of innumerable leaves, and a pattering as of the rain, and a whistling and a sighing like that of shrill winds singing in

the hollow canes, and wandering at night-time with a melancholy murmur in the creaking branches of the Dewadárus on the sides of the Snowy Mountain, mingled with a rushing like the water of a stream. And it rose and fell in waves, till it dinned in my ears like the roar of a mountain torrent: and then again it died away, vanishing by slow degrees as it were into the distance, with a sweetness that brought the tears into my eyes, and I strained my ears to follow it and catch it as it went, in agony lest it should be gone. And so as I listened, lost in an ecstasy of sound, drowned as it were in the boom and the eddies, and the echoes of that wind-begotten strain, as if against my will, I closed my eyes. And at that very moment, I heard the old mime singing, if indeed it was he that sang. For the tones of some faint, far-off caressing voice blended and mixed and twined and twisted and rose and fell with the sound of the flute, and the drowsy spell of that sleepy music resembled the noise of humming bees, soothing the brain of a tired man, resting at noon by a roadside tree. And that sweet voice rocked my soul like a breeze, swinging it quietly to and fro, as it whispered into my ear: Far away over the Lord of Hills, buried in the deep soft northern snow, I know of a dark blue pool. Sing hey![1] for the haunt of the swan. And the pool was made of a single tear, that rolled from the eye of the Snowborn Maid, to see Love's body burned. Sing ho! for the haunt of the swan. And on its bank there grows a flower, a great dark beautiful purple flower, whose fellow cannot be found on earth. Sing hey! for the haunt of the

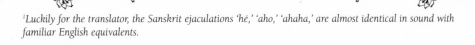

[1]*Luckily for the translator, the Sanskrit ejaculations 'hé,' 'aho,' 'ahaha,' are almost identical in sound with familiar English equivalents.*

swan. For it sprang from an accidental seed, that fell from Wishnu's 'párijáta' as he hurried across the sky. And the south wind caught and wafted it to the very edge of that snow-framed pool, and laid it there to grow. Sing ho! for the haunt of the swan. And it grew and grew and opened and bloomed, and loaded air with a scent that spoke of a half-remembered heaven. Sing hey! for the haunt of the swan. And every day out of the pool there comes to water that fragrant flower a spirit of the snow, holding high with round white arm on a great soft shoulder[1] a golden jar. Haha! the haunt of the swan. For Prakriti compounded her to serve that heavy-scented flower, and made her elementally of universal hues and stuffs and essences and shapes. And she spun her hair from the setting sun, a woof of dark red gold. Sing ho! for the haunt of the swan. And she painted her eyes with liquid blue drawn from a mountain tarn, and stained her lips with wet fresh ore, scarlet wrung out raw and pure from the very heart of the snowy rock. Sing hey! for the haunt of the swan. And she moulded her body of soft sea foam, and dyed her skin in vats of snow, and gave her an ear of an ocean shell. Haha! the haunt of the swan. And she stole her breast from the swell of the sea, and drew her hips from the great round hills, and went to creepers for her arms, and pliant canes for her slender waist. Sing ho! for the haunt of the swan. And she made her a soul of air and fire, and borrowed from the southern breeze the fragrance of her deep red hair, and went for the colour of the robe that drapes her silver body to her own great

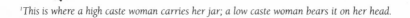

[1]*This is where a high caste woman carries her jar; a low caste woman bears it on her head.*

flower at eve. And slowly moves that great white woman, clasped in its purple folds, doubly bent as she moves along with the weight of her pitcher and her breast. Sing hey! for the haunt of the swan. Yellow and gold is her water pitcher, and hard and white is her milky breast. Sing ho! for the haunt of the swan. Does not the dusk of a starry night hide and shroud the round white hills? so are the limbs of that large-eyed lady wrapped in her own robe's purple folds. Haha! the haunt of the swan. And all around that lonely pool lie travellers that have been done to death, unable to endure the sweet and deadly poison of her kiss. Sing hey! for the haunt of the swan. For her kiss is like a snowflake's fall, sing ho! for the haunt of the swan; light and hardly to be felt, sing hey! for the haunt of the swan; and colder than the winter's moon, sing hey! for the haunt of the swan; and hotter than a burning flame, sing ho! for the haunt of the swan, and given to all who can find the way, Ha! ha! to the haunt of the swan.

And as the old mime sang, he raised his voice, louder and louder, till it ended in a roar that stunned my ears like a waterfall, sounding like a shout of laughter from the lips of the Great God. And as he ceased, I ran towards him. And I cried out: Ha! ha! the haunt of the swan. And then I fell at his feet in a swoon.

– Ha! Bhairawí,[1] art thou attentive? And the goddess answered: Dear Swan, speak on: I listen. And she caressed his snowy neck with the lotus of her hand.

[1]*The 'Terrible' one: a name of Párwatí.*

CHAPTER XI

O I lay there, I know not how long, drowned in the flood of that sudden swoon.[1] And when at last I came to myself, I saw all the officers of my household gazing at me with anxious eyes. But I saw no mime. Then I said sorrowfully: Alas! where is my mime? And a chamberlain came forward, and said: Maháraj, when we saw that that old deceiver had made thee also mad, like all the rest, and that for all that we could do, we could not bring thee to thyself, we laid hold of him, and carried him away again, and cast him into the river, to drown him. And lo! instead of drowning, that curious mime sank straight down into the water, pipe and all, like a stone, and never returned. And we fished for him with nets, but he was not there, and now we cannot tell what has become of him.

And then, with a shout, I rose up, and ran upon that unlucky chamberlain, and struck him to the ground. And I cried out: Slaves, you have destroyed him, and me also. And I fell upon them all, beating and striking them till they fled before me; and I handled them so, that at last they took counsel, and, led by the physicians, took me prisoner by force, and bound me; doing me no harm, but confining me to my bed, and setting over me a guard. And there for many days I lay, raving and struggling, and refusing to eat or drink, till I fell into a raging fever, and became as it were altogether mad. And in my delirium, I saw before me

[1]*A swoon is the conventional effect of all catastrophes, in Oriental stories. Those who live long in the East learn, that there is less exaggeration in this than at first sight would appear. Apathetic externally, the Hindoos, at least, are subject to sudden wild outbursts of emotional excitement that would astound the more phlegmatic European.*

nothing but a great white-armed woman, with hair that fell all round her like a shower of gleaming gold, seated by a purple flower the colour of her own clothes, and looking intently at me with half-shut colossal eyes, the colour of the pool by which she sat. And I wailed continually, like a sick child: Alas! the swan: alas! the swan. And the physicians flocked around me, utterly at a loss, vainly endeavouring to cure me by drugs and incantations and the letting me of blood. And finally they gave it up, saying to each other: He is entered and possessed by some demon,[1] and there is nothing to be done. And they left me to myself. And then there came a blank[2] and I remember absolutely nothing; for oblivion took me, like a nurse, into her arms, and I lay like a dead man in a long swoon,

And at last, after many days, I came back to myself. And yet, there was something of me that was wanting, left, as it were, behind. For I had utterly forgotten all the people round me: and I resembled a stranger, seeing all their new faces for the first time in my life. And I looked upon them all as enemies, saying to myself: Who are all these gaolers, that watch me, keeping me forcibly in prison? Now then, I must by all means manage to escape, and go very quickly to discover that haunt of the swan. For the tune of that old mime's song rang always in my head, and the gold-haired woman with her flower stood before me as if painted like a picture on my eyes, whenever I closed their lids. And therefore I lay, cunningly, still as death, without violence of any kind: till after a

[1] *The terrible old notion of possession – 'bhútawishta' – is an Indian idea: and depends on the theory of metempsychosis.*
[2] *Literally. an elision – 'lopa' –, the word grammatically employed to denote the cutting off a letter.*

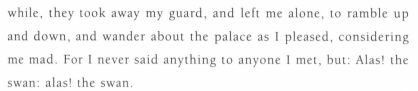

while, they took away my guard, and left me alone, to ramble up and down, and wander about the palace as I pleased, considering me mad. For I never said anything to anyone I met, but: Alas! the swan: alas! the swan.

And then, after a while, watching my opportunity, I stole out of the palace in the middle of the night. And I stepped noiselessly over the bodies of servants and watchmen, sleeping here and there; and I went down, and out into a garden, and found a little door in its wall, which I opened with a key. For through this very door I used formerly to pass, whenever I wished to leave the palace in disguise.

So I stood in the doorway of the open door, looking out. And as I did so, all at once I uttered a cry. And I exclaimed: Alas! alas! Here I am on the very point of starting on my journey, and yet I do not even know, which way to go.

And at that moment, I heard, just behind me, a faint sigh. And I started, as I heard it, saying to myself in terror: My gaolers have discovered me. And I turned, very quickly, and looked, and lo! before me was my wife.

– Ha! Windhyawásiní,[1] art thou attentive? And the goddess answered: Dear Swan, speak on: I listen. And she caressed his snowy neck with the lotus of her hand,

---

[1]*Dweller in the Windhya hills': a name of Párwati.*

CHAPTER XII

GAURÍ, I say, it was my wife: and yet, at the time, though I gazed at her, I knew not who she was. For all recollection of her,[1] as of the others, was utterly obliterated from my soul. And I said to her, sternly: Who art thou? Then she said: Dost thou not remember to have seen me before? And I said: No. – Alas! O Gaurí, now I know, what then I knew not: and doubtless she had watched me through my fever, and ever since: and dogging my footsteps, had followed me in the middle of the night. – And she laughed, and said: It is no matter who I am. And yet, know, that I am, of all the people in this city, the one whom, at this moment, thou wouldst most of all desire to see. And I looked at her, wondering who she was and what she meant. And after a while, she said again, in a low voice, as if she feared to be overheard: Thou art at this very moment about to start for the haunt of the swan. Say, is it not so? And I gazed at her in terror, and I debated within myself, whether I should not seize her by the throat and kill her, lest she should go and tell the others and prevent my escape. And presently I said: Thou art right: I am on the very point of starting: and what is that to thee? And she said: I know the way.

And when I heard, I was suddenly filled with a flood of joy, and could scarcely believe my ears. And in my delight, I was ready to take her in my arms; but hastily she shrank away. And I exclaimed:

[1] *This forgetfulness is part of the 'machinery' of Indian story tellers and dramatists: even European readers will recollect it in Shakuntalá.*

Thou art the very fruit of my birth in a female form. But who in the world art thou, to know the way? And she answered: Who I am, I cannot tell thee: for now I have abandoned the straight and narrow path of female conduct; and like a chariot, whose wheel has left the rut, I have run out of the course, by assuming independence. And yet it has been of necessity, and not of choice. And she sighed; and said again: Know this much only, that I am a wife whose husband has abandoned her, beguiled, as thou hast been thyself, by that old mime. And he left me, utterly forgetting me, for the sake of some marvellous unknown beauty that lives far off in the haunt of the swan. So finding him gone, I went to the mime, and said: Tell me the way to go, and that quickly; otherwise I will curse thee, and thy head shall instantly split in two.[1] And he, fearing my curse, told me: and now, if thou wilt, I will lead thee also.

So she spoke, deceiving me; and I, in my folly, was utterly deceived, so great was my desire to reach my goal. Ha! who can fix the limit of a woman's cunning, when love is her prompter and her spur? And I said: Come, then, and let us make forward, without loss of time, before the morning breaks, and my absence is discovered: for then certainly they would stop me. And together we went out, and closed the door. And I said to her:

Which way shall we go? Then she said: There. And she pointed to the Seven Rishis,[2] shining, away before us. And she said: We must go northward, and still northward, till we come to the place where the ways divide.

[1]*Cursing is only another form of prayer: and of curses, that of a pure woman was particularly to be dreaded, if we may credit our authorities.*
[2]*The Great Bear.*

And all at once, she began to sob. And I looked on her with compassion, and I said: Courage, O thou deserted lady. For many have crossed the sea of separation, and met again: and doubtless thou shalt find thy husband, away at thy journey's end.

And I gazed at the road, lying before us in the moonlight, white and still. And it ran out, long and thin, far away into the night, until its end was lost. And as I looked, I said to myself: Long, long is the high road: and yet, the end must come at last, And I turned to my wife and said: Come, And she said, in a low voice: Go thou on before, and I will follow.

So we went out upon the road, I first: and she followed, just behind[1].'

– Ha! Ambika,[2] art thou attentive? And the goddess answered: Dear Swan, speak on: I listen. And she caressed his snowy neck with the lotus of her hand.

[1]*In India, when a man and woman walk together, he goes first, and she follows, a step or two behind, with veiled head. And I never see them so, without thinking of Proudhon's admirable remark, that man comes down the ages, with woman attending him, 'pone sequens.' Those very foolish people who are at present trying to make them walk abreast fail, as Plato did, to perceive, that when masculine and feminine are reduced to neuter, life loses all its charm.*
[2]*The 'Mother': a name of Párwati.*

CHAPTER XIII

ND then, day and night, and night and day, together we went on, along the dusty road, which lengthened ever out before us, till it seemed to be indeed without an end. And whenever we were tired, we rested by the roadside. And here too, but for my wife, I should have ended my journey almost as soon as it began: for she had remembered, as I had forgotten, all. For when we were hungry, we should have starved, had she not foreseen it, and brought with her costly ornaments and jewels, one of which, every now and then, she broke as we went along, and sold it by pieces in the cities that we came to and passed through, and so purchased food. And thus we went on slowly, unnoticed, among so many other travellers and pilgrims,[1] and all the while I saw nothing that we passed, devoured as I was with desire to arrive at that haunt of the swan, and seeing nothing but that white armed beauty and her flower and her pool, with the song of that old mime ringing for ever in my ears as I listened to the wind in the trees. And I went on ever, like a man in a dream, paying hardly any attention to my companion, and living within myself: and every time we stopped, chafing, and almost crying with impatience, which robbed me of any feeling of fatigue. And every time she soothed me, and nursed me as though I were a child, singing me asleep, and telling me stories, and using every means to make me forget my impatience

[1] *India is, even now, full of pilgrims travelling in all directions.*

and the way. And all the while we went, day by day she grew thinner and weaker, and I saw it; and yet I paid no heed to it, thinking only of proceeding. And at length, she could no longer walk quickly, nor indeed at all, save a very little at a time, and she stopped to rest herself as it were at every moment.

So then, after a while, I said to myself: This is altogether unendurable, for we go so slowly, that the termination of my life will come upon me, before we reach the journey's end. And yet I cannot leave her behind, and go alone, being as it were tied to her, by reason of my ignorance of the way. And therefore I must somehow or other extract from her the secret: and then I shall be free.

And one day, as we rested by the road, I said: O thou easily tired one, if we stop in this manner every moment, we shall never get along. And what is the necessity for travelling together, since our objects are entirely distinct? Tell me, then, the way; so that I may go on before thee, and without thee, and make haste. Then said my wife: Alas! I cannot tell thee, till we have arrived at the place where the ways divide. And I said: Where, then, do they divide, and what is the reason why thou canst not tell me? Then she said: Be patient: now we shall very soon be there. But till we get there, I must not and will not tell thee. For that old mime, from whom I learned the way, forbade me, saying: I will return thee curse for curse. For as thou didst lay me under a curse, if I did not tell, so will I lay thee under another, if thou dost. The day, therefore, that thy tongue shall tell anyone the way, shall be the day of thy death. And

therefore it is that I only show to thee the way, but cannot tell.

So she spoke, in the cunning of her love, deceiving me again. But I looked at her with anger: and I said to myself: What does it matter to me, whether she live or die, provided only that I know the way? And from that moment, I behaved to her with harshness, looking upon her as the cause of my delay. And I began to hate her; and I hurried her along, refusing to stop, or let her stop, till she absolutely sank down, utterly unable to proceed; and I treated her with cruelty, blinded as I was by anger and by passion, so that I did not perceive that I was killing her. And I turned, as it were, my back upon her, treating her as if she were my enemy: and all the while she, on her side, took all my ill-behaviour with humility, as if she had deserved it. Alas! very terrible is the cruelty of those whose minds are blinded by the pursuit of a single object, and darkened by selfishness and passion. Thus do they fall at last into the hell of lower births, as has been the case with me.

– Hal Umá,[1] art thou attentive? And the goddess answered: Swan, speak on: I listen. And she took away from his neck the lotus of her hand.

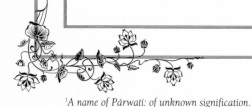

[1] *A name of Párwatí: of unknown signification.*

CHAPTER XIV

O we continued to go on, and every day my wife became more feeble, and I more brutal; and at last, one night, as I was urging her along, she fell down, as it were almost fainting, under a great 'ashwatta' tree that grew by the side of the road. And seeing her lying, I broke out into fierce abuse. And I exclaimed: Thou art the cause of my unhappiness, and now I am the victim of thy selfishness. Am I to perish, because thou wilt not tell me my road, in thy anxiety to preserve thy own miserable life? Then she said, gently: It is but a little way now. For if I am not mistaken, we have all but come to the very place where the ways divide. And she leaned with closed eyes against the trunk of the tree, and so remained, like one in a swoon. But I, in my frenzy, threw myself upon the ground, at a little distance, and lay; and there, after a while, sleep overtook me, for we had come many miles since the morning, in the heat of the sun.

And in the middle of the night, I awoke; and at that moment, I listened, and I heard her, crooning and singing as it were to herself, alone with the moon. And she said: Alas for me, and alas for him, and alas for the things that are all forgotten! O tyrant Love, had I done thee harm in a former birth, that thou hast selected me in this as a specimen of thy persecution? Lo! I am burned up in thy flame, and become as it were like a lotus flower, trodden under the careless foot of a forest elephant, to whom it had offered itself in vain. But now, O Love, I shall escape thee, for I have taken final refuge in the arms of a stronger God than thee. Thou hast been to me a poison, but Death shall be to me a medicine, cooler and more delicious than the rays of yon cold moon. O Death, thou art more merciful than bitter heartless Love, and now I transfer to thee my homage. For by thy aid, I have won my battle, and stolen as it were the march upon my rival of the purple flower; and long before he is with her, I shall be safe with thee.

And as I listened, I said to myself: She is mourning for her husband. And suddenly I rose up, and went towards her. And I said roughly: Come, rise: it is time to go. And she looked at me with dreamy eyes, for still she was leaning against the tree, and I think she had never moved, since I saw her last before I slept. And she said slowly: Thou art right: it is time: for thee, and for me also. And now, as I told thee, we have come to the place where the ways divide.

And I looked at her in perplexity. And I said: Art thou dreaming? Here there is no division of the road, which runs straight on, single and alone, into the dark of the night. Then she said: That is thine: but here, mine turns aside. And now, then, I will tell thee the way. And if, as thou goest, thou shouldst chance upon my husband, give him this, from me.

And all at once, she rose up, very quickly, with a great effort. And before I knew what she was doing, she put up her arms, and clasped my neck, and kissed me. And as she did so, I felt her arms

grip me like a cord, and her body shook all over. And suddenly, she let go, and fell back again against the tree.

And I said in astonishment: What is this, and what dost thou mean? And she looked up at me, and suddenly she began to laugh. And she said: Thy memory is of the shortest. Go on now: for thy way is open before thee. Now thou canst go on alone, and I have told thee all I know, about the way. And again I said: What way? And she said: Find it now, without me, and I can tell thee nothing more: for learn, that I know the way no better than thou dost thyself.

And I gazed at her, stupefied with the extremity of amazement. And I said: What! Hast thou, then, deceived me, and led me on, all this time, pretending to know the way, that all the time thou didst not know?

And she looked at me, with steady eyes, and answered: Yes.

– Ha! Bhawáni,[1] art thou attentive? And the goddess answered: Swan, speak on: I listen. And she stroked his snowy neck no more, looking at him with angry eyes.

[1] *A name of Párwatí: probably a feminine relating to 'Bhawa,' the Lord, who is.*

CHAPTER XV

ND I stood there for a moment, gazing at her silently, scarcely crediting my own ears. And I said to myself: I am cheated: and now this woman has ruined me, and led me utterly astray. And all at once, rage flowed in upon my soul, and almost burst my heart. And with a scream, I threw myself upon her, and caught her by the throat. And I shook her like a leaf, I know not how long, grasping her throat in a grip like that of death: and suddenly I flung her from me, and turned, and fled away, hardly knowing what I did, along the road, alone. So I ran on in the moonlight, till at last from sheer exhaustion I could absolutely run no more, while my soul was filled within me with the blackness of despair.

And all at once, I stopped, and stood. And I said to myself: What am I doing, and where is the advantage of rushing on at full speed, not even knowing whether I am going in the right direction? Alas! I have been all befooled by this execrable incarnation of deception, masquerading in a woman's shape; and now I am like nothing but a little drop of water in the very middle of the sea, to which all ways are alike. And all my labour has gone for nothing. Alas! alas! Who will bring me to the haunt of the swan?

And I looked round in the silence, seeing as it were the objects round me for the first time. And I saw that I was utterly alone in the dark plain, through which the road ran, clear and white and

without an end, as if to mock me, like a chain of silver on a sable robe. And I looked towards the east, and saw the pale dawn glimmering on the very edge of the world, as if preparing with apprehension to mingle with the moonlit night. And at that moment, I looked, and lo! there stood on the road beside me that very same old mime, exactly as he stood beside me in my palace hall, before.

And as I gazed at him in terror, my hair stood straight up on my head. And then, all at once I uttered a terrible cry. And I exclaimed: Ha! so thou art here again. Thou shalt not escape me, this second time.

Then that old mime looked at me, with dreadful eyes, and he said slowly: Thy memory is of the shortest. And as he spoke, I shuddered, and started, for he used her very words. And as I stood staring at him, like a picture painted on a wall, he said again with a mocking smile: Art thou, then, so sure, that we have met only once before? Is this only the second time?

And even as he spoke, that old mime disappeared: and in his place, there stood before me the old ascetic, at whom my wife had laughed, when he pricked his foot with a blade of grass. And he said: Dost thou not remember me, or is thy recollection still at fault? And I looked at him, amazed. And as I did so, once again he disappeared: and I saw before me the old Bhikshu, who met me with my father long ago, before the palace gates. And he said to me, very slowly: O child, born in the shadow of a sin, didst thou

[1] *A name of Párwati.*

imagine thou couldst escape the ripening of the fruit of the creeper of crime?

And then again, he was gone: and I was left alone. And as at first, I saw before me nothing but the empty road.

And at that very instant, I woke as it were from a long dream. And memory rushed suddenly back like light into my soul. And I cried out: Haha! haha! she was my wife; it was my wife. And all the while she stood beside me, and yet I did not know her. And like a madman, I have been running after phantoms, and now I am her murderer. And there came over me suddenly a horror, that lifted my hair from my body: and unable to endure it, all at once I fell to the ground, struck by the thunderbolt of remorse and grief. So I lay in the road, like a dead man, while day slowly came back into the world.

And then again, after a long while, I started to my feet. And I struck my hands together, crying aloud: What if she were not dead? Still, still there may be time.

– Ha! Kátyáyaní,[1] art thou attentive? And the goddess answered: Dear Swan, speak on: I listen. And once more she caressed his snowy neck with the lotus of her hand.

[1]*Water is offered to the spirits of the dead.*

CHAPTER XVI

ND then I began to run. And as I ran, I sobbed and wept, heaping curses on myself for my delay, and saying within myself: Had I only started sooner, I might have been in time. Alas! my memory is of the shortest. And I laughed aloud in my despair, and ran on, rent as it were in pieces by bitter grief and wild laughter and horrible apprehension, for well I knew she would be dead, and yet I thirsted with fierce desire to find her still alive. And I ran on as it were in a swoon, hardly conscious I was running, but with a soul whirling with passionate strain for a single object, to reach the place where I had left her. So I ran, sobbing, till the sweat fell from my limbs like rain, blinding me, dropping from my hair into my eyes; and my heart began to break within me, and my breast to choke and gasp for breath. And all at once I saw away on the road before me the great tree standing where she fell. And at the sight, my speed and strength returned to me. And I ran as if with wings, and reached that tree, and looked, and lo! there lay my wife still, exactly as I threw her down. And with a shout, I ran towards her, and threw myself on the ground beside her, and took her in my arms. And instantly, I shuddered at the touch of her: for she was cold: and she was a body without a soul.

And I let her fall to the ground, and stood up. And with both hands, I tore my hair out of my head, and stooping down, I heaped

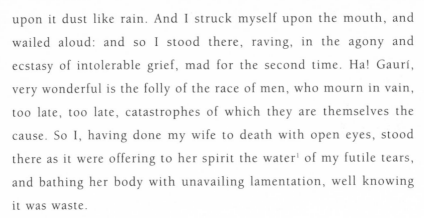

upon it dust like rain. And I struck myself upon the mouth, and wailed aloud: and so I stood there, raving, in the agony and ecstasy of intolerable grief, mad for the second time. Ha! Gaurí, very wonderful is the folly of the race of men, who mourn in vain, too late, too late, catastrophes of which they are themselves the cause. So I, having done my wife to death with open eyes, stood there as it were offering to her spirit the water[1] of my futile tears, and bathing her body with unavailing lamentation, well knowing it was waste.

So then, after awhile, I stooped, and sat down on the ground beside her, and lifted her on my knee. And I began to speak to her, as if she were alive. And I said: Come, it is but a little while, since thou didst strain thy dear arms about this worthless neck. Haha! my memory is very short, yet well do I remember how close was thy embrace. And in return for it, I slew thee. Now, put them round again. And I strove to make them meet once more around my neck, but they refused, standing out straight and stiff, like branches of a dry tree. And I wept again, holding her, cold as she was, close to my heart, and chattering in vain to her, with words that had no meaning, even had she been alive.

And at the last, I rose up, lifting her in my arms. And I said: Come, now, we will go on together as before. Yet not upon my road, either one way or the other. Didst thou not say thyself, that here the ways divided, and that thy way turned aside? Ha! rogue, thou didst deceive me: but now we will go together, along this

thorny way. And I turned off the road, and entered the jungle, and pushed through its pathless trees and branches, carrying my dead wife in my arms. So we went on together, while the thorns and branches tore me, yet I felt them no more than did my wife. And sometimes I stumbled, and we fell together to the ground; and always I picked her up again, and we went on as before. And all the while, the sun rose higher and higher into the sky, as if to follow us and watch. And so we went on, and all the while I talked to her: and all at once, we came upon a little pool of water, lying hidden as it were among the trees.

And at the sight, I let my wife suddenly drop upon the ground: and I began to clap my hands. And I exclaimed: Ha! after all, we have arrived, and beyond a doubt, this is that very haunt of the swan. And now I know what to do. And after all, my wife was right, and has led me well, and wisely: and I have found the object of my search, on her way, not my own. And doubtless the deity himself has guided, unknown to me, my footsteps to this pool.

And then, very quickly, I knelt beside my wife. And shaking loose her long dark hair, I tied it round my neck, so tightly that it almost choked me. And then I took her in my arms, and going to the pool, I leaped with her into its cold dark water. And together we sank down into its depths, and so we reached another birth. And by the favour of the deity no doubt it was, that we were born again a pair of swans.

A MIME OF DEITY

A MIME OF DEITY

ND at that very moment, there rang in the air the scream of a swan. And instantly, the swan exclaimed: Ha! there is my wife, calling to me to come to her. O Gaurí, fare thee well: for now my time is up, and I must go. And he left the water, and rose up soaring into the blue air, and flew away, answering his mate with loud screams.

And the Daughter of the Mountain called after him: Stay! O swan, return, and bring me thy wife to see. But the swan, paying her no attention, disappeared over the hill. And as the goddess gazed after him, suddenly the bee also started from her bosom, and exclaimed: O Gaurí, I am warmed, and I too have a wife. And in a moment, he also flew away. And the snake slid from her neck, and glided silently away, and was lost along the ground. And the bear said politely: O Durgá, surely that swan was a good story-teller, but a very bad husband: and now I will not be, like him, the destruction of my family: therefore I take leave of thee, with a coat sanctified by the touch of thy lotus foot. And he trotted away, over the hill; and the Daughter of the Mountain was left alone.

And she looked round, and said sadly to herself: See how all these husbands go quickly to their wives. I only am forsaken. And tears from the well of self-commiseration rose up into her eyes. And at that moment, she heard behind her a noise of steps. And she looked and saw, coming towards her, a great white bull.[1]

[1] *Nandi is Shiwa's vehicle.*

And instantly, she ran to him, and put her arm around his mighty neck. And she said, leaning against his side, and hiding her face against his hump: O Nandi, dear Nandi, I am most miserable.

And Nandi put round his huge head, as she leaned against him, and licked her ancle with his tongue. And he bellowed, very gently, and said, in deep tones: How should the Mistress of the World be miserable? Then said Párwatí: Alas! mistress though I be, I am, notwithstanding, deserted by the world.[1] And as she spoke, she felt Nandi changing as she leaned against him; and she looked up quickly, and uttered a cry. For Nandi was gone, and she was leaning against the Great God. And she hung her head, blushing as she did so. And the moon-crested god took her in his arms, and said, looking at her with affection: O wayward one, thy memory is of the shortest.

And instantly, that sister of the snowflake started, looking at him in amazement. Then said the god with a smile: Hast thou then forgotten that our parting was thy doing and not mine? Or didst thou think the World would ever be absent from his mistress, even for a moment? Know, that I was with thee all the time. For I was the swan, that stole from thee caresses by telling thee a tale, and I was the bee, that rested on thy breast, and I was the snake, that twined myself about thy neck, and I was the bear, that lay near thee to support thy foot: and again I was Nandi, against whom thou didst lean. And thus all the while I penetrated in disguise the

[1]*Observe that 'world' here means also the Great God – 'bhawa.'*

armour of thy anger, and was caressed by thee against thy will. And know, moreover, O Daughter of the cold white hill, that thy anger was without a cause. For Gangá is my attribute: and even I could not exist without my proper attributes. But thou art my wife, and the other half of me.

And as he spoke, he gave that beautiful one[1] a kiss. And instantly he said: Ha! thou art very cold, even for a child of the snow. And the goddess shivered a very little, and said: I have been sitting for so long, motionless and silent, by this cold pool. And moreover, my heart was ice, within me, for I was, as I imagined, away from thee.

Then said the Great God: See!

And the Daughter of Himálaya looked up, and as she did so, there came a change over the pool. For the cold air suddenly became warm, and the water suddenly changed colour, and its blue altered from black to pale, and its lotuses suddenly blushed with red, and great trees suddenly appeared around it, and bushes started out around them, and suddenly burst forth into blossom, loading the warm breeze that fanned them with fragrance of the champak and the mango and the sandal and the south. And innumerable bees hummed about those magic flowers, and beautiful birds like emeralds and rubies floated and sang about the trees: and it was, as though time had been annihilated, and Winter suddenly overtaken and ousted, in the twinkling of an eye, by Spring.

[1]*This may also mean his left half – 'wama.' Wamika is a name of Párwatí, including a pun.*

And the goddess said, with wonder in her lotus eyes: This is thy doing, O moony-crested: and all these fair flowers with their fragrance are illusion, and unreal. Then said Maheshwara: O simple one, this illusion differs only from reality in that it will not last so long. For what is Time, but I myself?[1] and what are the worlds but mere illusion, and a thing, like these flowers, produced for my diversion, and a play, of which I am myself the sole and only mime? For as in the case of the swan, and all thy other late companions, it is I who am the background and the only true reality, and all they are only shapes, images[2] and phantoms and appearances of me.

And even as he spoke, there came to the edge of that Mánasa lake an old pilgrim, who had travelled all his life to reach it and die in its vicinity. But the Great God was aware of his arrival, as he drew near. And as that old pilgrim looked towards them, he saw neither god nor goddess, but only a pair of royal swans, billing each other on the edge of that cold lake.

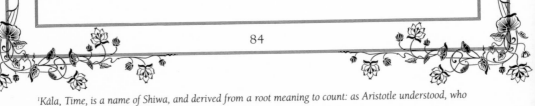

[1]*Kála, Time, is a name of Shiwa, and derived from a root meaning to count: as Aristotle understood, who understood everything.*
[2]*'Pratíka.'*

HERE ENDS
AN INCARNATION OF THE SNOW,
TRANSLATED FROM THE
ORIGINAL MANUSCRIPT
BY F. W. BAIN